PRESENTED BY

Kate and David Armstrong
in honor of
Dorothy Armstrong
1998

SMYTHE GAMBRELL
LIBRARY

WESTMINSTER SCHOOLS

ANCIENT EGYPTIAN PEOPLE

by Sarah McNeill

The Millbrook Press
Brookfield, Connecticut

For Tobie

Published in the United States in 1997 by

The Millbrook Press
2 Old New Milford Road
Brookfield, Connecticut 06084

First published in Great Britain in 1996 by

Wayland Publishers Ltd. incorporating MacDonald Young Books
61 Western Road
Hove
East Sussex
BN3 1JD

Designed by Neil Adams
Illustrations by Philip McNeill
Consultant: Joanna Defrates

Text copyright © 1996 Sarah McNeill
Illustrations copyright © Philip McNeill

Typeset by DP Press Ltd, Sevenoaks, Kent

Printed and bound by Proost International Book Co., Belgium

Library of Congress Cataloging-in-Publication Data

McNeill, Sarah
Ancient Egyptian people / Sarah McNeill
  p. cm.
Includes bibliographical references and index.
Summary: Describes the everyday lives of thirteen ancient Egyptian people
through the use of quotations and illustrations of the time.
ISBN 0-7613-00562 (lib. bdg.)
1. Egypt--Civilization--To 332 B.C. --Juvenile literature.
[1. Egypt--Civilization--To 332 B.C.] I Title
DT61.H65 1997
932--dc20

96-3576
CIP
AC

Picture Acknowledgments

Picture research by Image Select, London

Front cover: Image Select, London; Spine: Spectrum Colour Library; AKG: pp 40,
44; Ancient Art & Architecture Collection: Contents page, pp 8, 10, 13, 16, 17, 18,
21, 22, 23, 27, 31, 33, 38, 43; Ann Ronan Picture Library: pp 7, 24, 25, 29, 45;
Bridgeman Art Library: pp 15, 35; Image Select, London: Title page, p 9; Spectrum
Colour Library: pp 6, 11, 14, 20, 42; Werner Forman Archive: pp 12, 19, 26, 28, 30,
32, 34, 36, 37, 39, 41

CONTENTS

INTRODUCTION

Imagine that you had to tell someone from another planet about the world in which we live today. How would you do it? One way would be to think of different sorts of people and the work they do. In this way, you could sum up everything, from politics to family life.

Now imagine this. Nearly 5,000 years ago, one of the world's first great civilizations grew up on the banks of the Nile River in Egypt. If, all those years ago, a group of Egyptians had sat down to draw up a list of people who were important to them, who would they have thought of? They would have put their all-powerful king, pharaoh, and his officials at the top of their list. Then they would have added people who served the gods, or helped to prepare the dead to live forever – priests, mummy-makers and tomb-builders, for example. People such as these were either rich and powerful, or educated and highly skilled. Poor hard-working people, such as the peasants, would have seemed much less important to the Egyptians, even though they made a big contribution to everyday life.

In the pages that follow, you can find out about all these different sorts of people – rich and poor, male and female – who helped to create the great civilization of ancient Egypt.

THE PHARAOH

O f all the people in ancient Egypt, pharaoh was the most important. He was an all-powerful king. This is how an Egyptian nobleman named Rekhmire summed up pharaoh's power, about 3,500 years ago:

What can I say about the king of Egypt? He gives everyone safety. He is like a father and mother to all people. No one can equal pharaoh.

The first pharaohs

The land of Egypt was ruled by pharaohs from about 3000 B.C. until Roman times (around 30 B.C.). The first pharaohs brought about a big and important change in Egypt. It became one country, ruled by one king. Until about 3000 B.C., the land had been divided in two: Upper Egypt, which lay to the south, and Lower Egypt, which lay to the north. Each had its own ruler. Then a king from the south turned the whole land into his kingdom. Historians are not sure which king was responsible for this, although Egyptian legends tell of a powerful king called Menes who was such a conqueror. Whatever the truth of the legends, it is certain that from this time onward, Egypt was a mighty and prosperous land, ruled by all-powerful pharaohs.

All-powerful kings

Egypt was one of the first countries ever to have such a powerful king. You can tell just how powerful pharaoh was

Pharaoh Seti I (1306–1290 B.C.) triumphant over his enemies in battle. Seti is shown as a huge figure who towers over all the other people in the picture. Egyptian artists presented their king in this way to show how important he was.

from the story of one high-ranking Egyptian priest. The priest was on such good terms with pharaoh that he was given a special privilege when they met: *"His Majesty allowed me to kiss his foot."* Any other Egyptian would have had to kiss the ground!

Pharaoh's subjects were expected to obey him without question. In very early times, pharaoh's servants and courtiers had to be prepared to die when pharaoh died. Archaeologists have found evidence that hundreds of royal servants were put to death and buried alongside their royal masters, but this ritual soon stopped. Model figures or drawings made on the walls were buried instead.

A group of Africans arriving with gold for pharaoh. Many pharaohs were eager to import luxury goods from abroad. A ruler called Hatshepsut (1473–1458 B.C.) was especially famous for being interested in trading with other lands. Hatshepsut was famous for another reason too – she was a woman. Most pharaohs were men.

Living god

The people of Egypt had many gods – and pharaoh was one of them. Pharaoh was especially identified with one of the gods, called Horus, who was pictured with the head of a hawk. Pharaoh was also thought to be the son of the sun god, Re, the most important of all the gods.

As a living god, pharaoh was believed to be responsible for almost everything – from rainfall to the harvest. One inscription proclaimed:

If you say to the water "Come upon the mountain," the waters of heaven will burst out.

These words show how firmly the Egyptians believed their king had supernatural power. Pharaoh was also expected to maintain good relations between his people and the other gods. He had to build temples to the gods, and see that the gods were properly worshiped. He had many other responsibilities, too. He was expected to protect his people, keep law and order, and defend the land against its enemies in time of war. To do all these things, pharaoh needed help. He appointed large numbers of officials to see to the everyday running of the country – making sure that the harvest was safely gathered in and that the country had supplies of food, and checking that people paid their taxes.

To kill the king

In very early Egyptian history, a king whose power began to fail because he was old or ill was seen as a danger to his people. He could no longer guarantee protection from the gods, and so he had to die. But in the days of the pharaohs, there were special magic ceremonies which were thought to revive pharaoh's power, and so kings were no longer sacrificed.

The ultimate prize

Being pharaoh had one very important reward. The king was thought to live on with the gods when his earthly body died. In time, all Egyptians claimed that they could live forever. But at first, it was only the king who had this ultimate prize. Pyramids and splendid tombs were built to help protect his body on its way to the gods.

THE PEASANT

Many people took a gloomy view of the peasant's life. One Egyptian put it like this:

The farmer spends eight hours ploughing. He eats half the crop and a hippopotamus eats the rest. And mice ... locusts ... Even cattle eat the harvest – and sparrows steal it!

The world's first farmers

Although they didn't know it, the peasant farmers of ancient Egypt were carrying on a way of life that made history.

The first people to live in the area that became known as Egypt did not live by farming. They were hunters, fishermen, scavengers, who depended on catching fish and wild animals or gathering wild plants for their food. They did not live in one fixed place, but followed the animals as they roamed the land. We call this a "hunter-gatherer" way of life. Then came a move toward greater control of the environment: planting crops such as wheat, waiting

An Egyptian peasant drives a plow pulled by oxen. This model was made for a tomb in about 2000 B.C. When the tomb owner died, the model was expected to come to life and work, so that the dead person would have enough to eat in the afterlife.

for them to grow and then harvesting them, as well as taming animals and raising them for food. All of this pointed to a new, settled lifestyle. Historians think that this change began to take place in Egypt in about 12000 B.C., and that it was one of the first places on earth where people made the shift from being hunter-gatherers to being farmers. The change did not happen all at once, and it was probably from about 5000 B.C. onward that farming really became important in Egypt.

Great river god

Farming in the hot, dry land of Egypt depended on water, and water had to come from the great Nile River. Each year, in the middle of July, the Nile would start to flood. These floods left thick, black mud all over the country-

side. This mud was ideal for growing crops – and as soon as the floods subsided, that is exactly what the peasant farmers did. Wheat, barley, flax, vegetables and fruit – such as dates, grapes, and figs – all grew abundantly. Every Egyptian, from the poorest peasant to the nobles at pharaoh's court, knew that without the regular Nile flood there would be no food crops. It was no wonder that they believed the Nile was controlled by one of the gods, Hapy.

The people in this painting are not peasants; instead it shows a tomb builder named Sennedjem and his wife. This couple did no farm work when they were alive, but, like other Egyptians, they believed they would have to help in the fields in the life after death. This painting would do the work for them.

Food for everyone

It was not just farming that the River Nile made possible, it was a whole way of life – for the peasants and everyone else in Egypt. Because crops did so well, the peasants could grow more than they needed for themselves. This meant that not

A peasant looking after cattle. Cattle were very valuable – so valuable that their owners liked to have paintings of them in their tombs.

everyone had to work as a peasant growing food. People were free to do other jobs – as craftsmen or priests, for example. It also meant that some people, such as pharaoh and his courtiers, could live in leisure and luxury, doing no hard physical work at all, because the peasants would provide everything they needed.

"Alas for the farmer!"

Just as everyone depended on the Nile River, so they depended on the hard work of the peasants. But the peasants received little reward for their back-breaking work. They owned no land of their own: it all belonged to pharaoh, and to the temples and nobles to whom pharaoh made gifts. When harvest time came around, it was the land owner who was given the largest share of the crops, not the peasant. Paintings from Egyptian tombs show us what happened if land owners did not get all the crops they wanted: the peasant was beaten with a stick. *"Alas for the farmer!,"* sighed one ancient writer sympathetically.

In early times, it was not only farm work that was expected of the peasants. While the Nile was flooding each year, pharaoh called his people up to work on great building projects, such as temples, tombs, and pyramids.

THE PRIEST

Religion was very important to the Egyptians. So when pharaoh chose someone to serve the gods as an important priest, he wanted everyone to know it. This is how Pharaoh Ramses II (1290–1224 B.C.) announced a new priest to serve the god, Amun:

Nebunef has been named high priest of Amun. The king has sent his messenger to inform the whole land [about this].

Permitted to see the gods

The Egyptians believed in about 2,000 gods and goddesses. Each was supposed to have different powers. The god Osiris, for example, was lord of the dead, as well as crops and fertility. Gods came in all sorts of shapes and sizes, many in human bodies with animal heads. The goddess Hathor was thought to have a woman's body and cow's horns, and Sobek a crocodile's head and man's body.

Some priests and priestesses were required to make offerings of food and drink to the dead. Here, you can see offerings being brought by servants for just this purpose.

To worship the gods, the Egyptians built temples, where the gods' spirits were supposed to live. Few people, except the priests and priestesses, were permitted inside the temples. Pharaoh was allowed inside to "see" the gods, because he was thought to be a god himself. He was the high priest of all Egypt. It was his duty to make sure that the gods were worshiped properly. Pharaoh did this by choosing men to serve as priests and women to serve as priestesses.

Working in the temple

Priests usually served in temples dedicated to gods, and priestesses in temples dedicated to goddesses. They wore distinctive dress: especially important priests wore leopard skin robes, for example. The temples were bustling places, filled with many priests, each with different duties. The most important priests and priestesses came from educated, high-ranking families who knew pharaoh well. These people were the "high priests." Below them came a whole range of lesser priests, including some who served only "part-time."

Looking after the dead was an important part of religion. Here, you can see a mummy on a couch with an embalmer bending over it. The embalmer wears a jackal mask to represent the god, Anubis.

Waking the gods

The priests' work centered on the statue of the god kept in each temple. It was treated not just as a statue, but as a living being. Each day ceremonies were held in its honor. As the sun rose, the god had to be awakened. A procession of the most senior priests made its way to the sanctuary at the heart of the temple where the statue was housed, to make offerings of food and drink to it. It was washed and dressed in fresh clothing. Water was sprinkled around it and incense was burned. Then the priests left, brushing away their footprints and taking care to close the doors and fasten them with a special seal made of clay, so that no one could break into the god's presence without permission.

Purification

Before they could take part in sacred ceremonies such as these, the priests had to purify themselves – inside and out. This meant shaving their bodies of all hair, bathing in a special pool in the precincts of the temple, and not eating certain foods, like salt. They even chewed pellets of natron, a chemical which was used to preserve dead bodies, to cleanse their insides.

Festival days

Once or twice a year, great festivals were held when statues were taken from the temples and carried out among the people. The priests had to carry the statue of the god and see to its safe journey. Pharaoh sometimes sent his officials to check on their work. Senwosret III (1878–1841 B.C.) did this when the priests of Osiris carried their statue from the temple at Abydos down the Nile in a special boat. *"I decorated the great ship. They followed the god and put on his finery. I concluded the Great Procession following the god in his steps,"* the official reported back.

A power in the land

Many temples, and their priests, became rich and powerful as pharaoh presented the gods with gifts. Land, jewels, precious metals, herds of animals, crops – all these were given to the temples by pharaoh. The priests of the god Amun at Thebes were especially important. When, in about 1353 B.C., a new pharaoh called Akhenaten (1353–1335 B.C.) announced that he was going to worship the sun god in a new way and closed all the temples except those dedicated to Aten (the visible sun disc), it was as if he were declaring war and an economic disaster. The priests of Amun made sure that the changes did not last for long.

Egyptian gods and goddesses made of gold. The god Osiris is in the middle. His wife, Isis, stands on the left-hand side and his son, Horus, on the right-hand side.

THE MUMMY-MAKER

The Egyptians did not want to die. They saw no reason why life should not carry on when they were dead – as long as all the right magic was on their side. So as the men who turned dead bodies into mummies set to work, they chanted magic spells like this one, to make everything go according to plan:

O flesh of the king, do not decay, do not rot, do not smell unpleasant!

Cheating death

Historians and scientists can use mummies like these to give us valuable clues about the health of people who lived in ancient Egypt. X-rays are very helpful. X-ray evidence shows that many Egyptians suffered from bone diseases like arthritis.

When they thought about what happened when they died, the Egyptians decided that there would be another life in store for them – a life lasting forever, just like their life on earth, with parties, hunting expeditions, games and good meals. But some preparations were needed first. They had to stay on the right side of the gods, and learn the correct magic spells. And still there was one big problem. This concerned their bodies.

The most important part of a person was thought to be his or her spirit, or double, known as the "ka."

Where was the ka going to live after death if its body rotted away? The answer was obviously that if the Egyptians wanted to cheat death, their bodies had to be carefully preserved, for all time. This was the job of the embalmers, the mummy-makers.

Making a mummy

Turning a corpse into a mummy was a magical and mysterious business. Everything had to be done in just the right way. A god called Anubis, who had the head of a jackal, was supposed to be in charge of the process. The embalmers wore jackal masks to show that they were doing Anubis' work, and to make sure that his power would flow through them.

First of all, the corpse was taken to the embalmers' workshop. The workshop had special magic names, such as the "House of Vigor" (strength). This name helped to make sure that embalming gave the dead body back its strength. As one spell put it:

Your flesh shall rise up for you! Your bones shall join together! Your flesh shall reassemble!

Once in the workshop, the body was cut open with a small incision in the side, and the internal organs were removed. Liver, stomach, intestines, and lungs were dried out and stored in special jars. The Egyptians thought that bad magic could be worked against you if an enemy got hold of any part of your body, even a single hair. So these internal organs would eventually be buried alongside the mummy for protection.

Next, the body had to be dried out. For 40 days it lay packed in crystals of a chemical called natron. At the end of this period it would have looked horrifying. It was time for the embalmers to restore as life-like an appearance as possible. They filled out the body cavities with packing and anointed the skin with a mixture of spices, milk, and wine.

An elaborate coffin made to house the mummy of a singer in the Temple of Amun. Coffins were painted with pictures of the gods and other scenes, including portraits of the dead person. Wealthy people had several coffins, one stacked inside the other. The final one was made of stone.

This painting on papyrus shows one of the rituals that took place when someone was buried. It is called the "opening of the mouth." You can see the family of the dead person mourning at the front of the tomb.

Artificial eyes were added, and perhaps a wig. Then the mummy-makers applied a coating of resin all over the body. For women, they added cosmetics and jewelry. Next came bandaging, a process lasting 15 days. Magic spells guided each step. Finally the embalmers added a special mask and placed the body in an elaborately decorated coffin. The mummy was now ready for burial.

On the way to eternal life

In early times, only pharaoh was thought to live forever. Tremendous efforts were made to preserve his body – not just by mummifying it, but by creating great pyramids to protect it and to house everything pharaoh would need to live in splendor in the next life. The great pyramid of Khufu (2551–2528 B.C.) is a good example. But after about 2040 B.C., the idea of an afterlife for everyone became accepted. Anyone who could afford it was to be mummified after death, with an elaborate funeral and a fine tomb to be buried in.

The climax of any funeral came when the mummy was propped at the door of its tomb, and a priest performed a ceremony known as the "opening of the mouth." This was thought to restore the body's powers: the magic moment that the embalmers had worked for.

THE VIZIER

The vizier was pharaoh's most important official. Words painted inside the tomb of a vizier named Rekhmire in about 1450 BC tell us about this much-honoured position:

'His Majesty said, "Be vizier! Look after everything." Being vizier is not easy.'

Looking after everything

One of ancient Egypt's great achievements was the way pharaoh managed to make people all over the country obey him. He did this by employing a large number of officials to work for him. Using a great network of officials to build up a powerful state was a revolutionary step for the time.

A vizier arrives in style, carried on a sort of ceremonial stretcher or litter called a palanquin. Only important people traveled this way.

The vizier was at the head of this network of officials. Historians believe that there were usually two viziers at work – one in Upper Egypt and one in Lower Egypt. Between them they supervised law and order, tax collection, and all sorts of trades and crafts. They also kept an eye on Egypt's defenses, and checked the work of all the other officials.

Pictures from the tomb of the busy Rekhmire show the vizier at work. Here are pharaoh's taxes – not in money, but in goods. There is honey from beehives, crops from the fields, cattle plodding along with their calves. There are statues from craftsmen's shops, too. Rekhmire has to record them all. Foreigners arrive with gifts for pharaoh from their kings. Rekhmire even has to record tributes and see that these are safely guarded. Then there are journeys around Egypt on official business. Frontier fortresses need inspecting. Craftsmen employed by pharaoh must be supervised, and the goods they make, from gold work to statues, carefully stored away in royal warehouses. This was what it meant to "look after everything."

Loved and praised by pharaoh

It was an honor to be appointed vizier. Only high-ranking, educated noblemen were likely to find themselves rewarded by pharaoh in this way. *"I was the one whom my lord loved and praised every day,"* one important official modestly remembered, looking back on his career. Throughout the land, everyone recognized the importance of pharaoh's viziers. The story of the world's first recorded strike, in about 1153 B.C., tells us about this. It took place in the Valley of the Kings, the great building site where tombs for the pharaohs were prepared by gangs of craftsmen. Wages were slow in coming, and the workers put down their tools. Who was the one they demanded to see? It was the vizier. *"There*

As well as the vizier, pharaoh was served by many other officials. This is a life-like statue of one of pharaoh's top servants – a man named Rahotep. Rahotep was an important courtier: a prince, a high priest, and an army officer. Skilled craftsmen made this painted stone statue for his tomb.

is no clothing, no ointment, no fish, no vegetables. Send to the vizier so provision may be made for us," ran their demands.

Never under guard

But as the words in Rekhmire's tomb remind us, it was not always easy being vizier. Noblemen were not always on good terms with pharaoh. Sometimes pharaoh and his nobles competed for power. One vizier, called Pepiankh, left a record in his tomb of difficult days: *"I never went to bed without taking my official seal. I was never put under guard. When anything was said against me, I was cleared."* Pepiankh knew that he might easily have been punished instead.

Struggles for power

Under strong and wise pharaohs, Egypt enjoyed long stretches of peaceful government. But there were some periods when government broke down and power struggles followed.

Egypt was divided into administrative areas called "nomes." Each one was ruled by a local governor called a "nomarch." When pharaoh's power grew weak, the nomarchs tried to increase their own influence. This happened at the end of the time that historians call the "Old Kingdom" (2575–2134 B.C.), and again between the end of the "Middle Kingdom" (2040–1640 B.C.) and the beginning of the "New Kingdom" (1550–1070 B.C.). At these times, strong rule by pharaoh and officials such as the vizier collapsed, leaving local nobles vying for power.

This painting shows craftsmen at work making jewelry. The man on the left is making a jeweled collar. The man on the right is using a drill to bore a hole in beads. The vizier was like a prime minister and was responsible for all of Egypt's craftsmen and workers.

THE SCRIBE

The word "scribe" means "one who writes." This is what one writing man, called Khety, wrote about his work in about 2000 B.C.:

It is the greatest of all jobs – there is no other job like it in all the land. See, there is no worker without a boss – except the scribe, who is always his own master. So if you can learn to write, it will be far better for you than anything else.

Writing – a revolution

Writing first developed in the area known today as the Middle East, in a place called Sumer (in what is today Iraq). This was a great communications revolution. It was not long before Egypt too began experimenting, and from about 3000 B.C. onward writing began to play a significant part in Egyptian life.

Scribes squatted or sat down to work, as this life-like statue shows us.

The development of writing meant that people could keep accounts and records of all kinds of things – such as how much grain came in from the harvest, who owed money to another person, what was stored in a warehouse. There were all sorts of uses for written records and reports. It was people with power, like pharaoh, who really benefited. Writing meant they could boost their power over the people, by sending out written commands and receiving written reports to find out what was going on all over the land.

Here, scribes are at work recording the grain collected at harvest time. This tomb painting tells us a good deal about the Egyptians and their daily lives. It also tells us about the work of Egyptian artists. Do you notice how they almost always paint people as if we were looking at them from the side?

The mysterious power of the scribe

As a new and secret skill, writing was the craft of only a few specially trained men – the scribes. Their skill was very much in demand. It set them apart as a group with special privileges. Unlike peasants and craftsmen, scribes didn't have to do hard physical work. They worked with pens and brushes, keeping cool and clean under the hot Egyptian sun. *"Become a scribe! Your hands will stay soft. You can wear white clothes. You will be so important that even courtiers will greet you."* This is how one Egyptian urged schoolboys to train as scribes.

There were other reasons, too, why men were interested in this career. It was a way of getting magical power. The Egyptians were very superstitious about words, believing that they had special power. One "cure" for snake bite, for example, involved this magical ceremony. A special spell was written down. Then water was poured over the writing, and the patient drank the water. The magic of the writing was thought to flow into the water, and then into the sufferer. Customs such as this show how the Egyptians almost worshiped writing. There was even a special god of writing and counting, known as Thoth. Thoth was shown with a human body and the head of a bird called an ibis, which had a very long beak shaped like a pen. All this evidence explains how the scribes, who could read and write, were set apart from other people.

Learning the job

Scribes learned their job from older, qualified men. Training started in boyhood, from about the age of

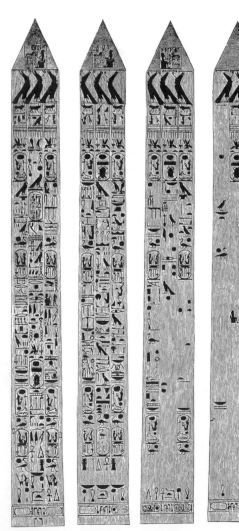

Hieroglyphics were used for formal purposes, such as writing carved on monuments. This obelisk (four-sided pillar) has hieroglyphics cut into each of its sides.

12. Once a boy had learned to write, he had to practice copying out exercises from special textbooks. A qualified scribe worked on rolls of writing material called papyrus, but trainees were not trusted with good-quality material. They were given pieces of broken pottery or flakes of limestone to practice on.

There was a lot to practice, because the Egyptians used more than one type of writing. For really important work, such as inscriptions in royal tombs, they used "hieroglyphics." These were elaborate signs, a combination of picture signs representing ideas and other signs representing sounds. For everyday use, there was "hieratic" writing, which was simpler. The difference between the systems was rather like the difference between printing and handwriting today. In later times, around 700 B.C., a third type of writing, called "demotic," was used too. This was also a kind of "handwriting."

THE ROBBER

I n these words, robbers thousands of years ago confessed to a daring theft from a temple in ancient Egypt:

We went yet again to the door and we brought away gold. We bought grain with it in Thebes and divided it up.

Cheats and robbers

All sorts of crimes took place in Egypt. Some were the same as those that take place anywhere, such as murder, stealing, and cheating at business. Others tell us about the special worries of the ancient Egyptians. These included building dams to stop people's fields from receiving their share of water from the flooding of the Nile River, and stealing offerings that were put in the temples for the gods. Both of these were thought of as serious

The ancient Egyptians took special precautions to try to make sure their burial places would not be robbed. These included placing stone "plugs" and gates in the pyramids to seal off all access. How do you think they would have reacted to the archaeologists and tourists who have been visiting their tombs for centuries?

crimes by the Egyptians. One of the very worst crimes of all was to rob the riches stored in pyramids and tombs built for the pharaohs. In the reign of Ramses IX (1131–1112 B.C.), several of these break-ins were discovered. The robber band confessed that mummies and jeweled coffins had been stolen.

To catch a thief

Although these robbers might have been daring, they still met with the moment that all law-breakers dreaded. They were caught. The powerful Egyptian state did not look kindly on anyone who broke the law. There were many laws and punishments intended to keep the country safe, and many officials with special powers to make sure the law was kept.

This Egyptian tried to avoid paying his taxes. You can see what happened to people who committed such crimes and were caught.

Anyone could make a complaint if they felt that they had been wronged. It didn't matter who you were – rich or poor – anyone could ask for justice. Even women were allowed to study law. In this respect they had the same rights as men. This was very unusual, and not just for ancient society because until very modern times, few countries have given women equal rights before the law. Each case came up before a law court, which was usually held close to where the people involved lived. The case was put before a local official called a magistrate, who decided what was to be done. More important cases were kept for the vizier to decide.

Facing the penalty

Justice could be very harsh. For some crimes, it was enough for the thief to give back the stolen goods and pay a fine. The fine was usually set at twice the value of what had been stolen. But the courts could give much more severe penalties. Beatings were a common punishment – 100 or even 200 blows with a cane, for example. Culprits were sometimes branded (burned with hot metal). The burn would show permanently, and was a sign that the person was not to be trusted.

Punishments like these were given by local courts for fairly ordinary crimes. People whose cases went to the vizier, or sometimes even to pharaoh himself, met with a far worse fate. Those who plotted against pharaoh, or were thought to have offended the gods, could be mutilated by having a hand, nose or ear cut off. Others were sentenced to work in mines or quarries far away in the desert. The most serious cases of all meant a penalty of death by drowning, burning, or being impaled on a post.

Offending the gods

The Egyptians believed that crime did not just upset law and order on earth. It also upset the general order of the universe controlled by the gods. The cosmic law and order that came from the gods was called "maat" (named for the goddess of truth and justice) and was thought to guide everything, from nature to people. Because criminals upset maat, the Egyptians expected the gods to punish them, too, with illness, poverty, and even death. Even after death, criminals could not escape, because the gods would put them on trial. A monster called Ammit, the Eater of the Dead, would be waiting to eat the heart of anyone found guilty.

This splendid collar, set with jewels, comes from the tomb of Tutankhamen (1333–1323 B.C.). The tombs of the royal family were like great treasure houses; even in ancient times their contents proved tempting for thieves. All the tombs in the Valley of Kings were robbed by 1000 B.C. – except Tutankhamen's.

THE CHARIOTEER

Ancient battle scenes were carved in many Egyptian temples. When Pharaoh Ramses II (1290–1224 B.C.) described in his temples his great battle with the army of the Hittite people at Kadesh (1274 B.C.), he singled out the chariots for attention:

His Majesty went to look about him and he found 2,500 chariots hemming him in.

Battle revolution

The chariot arrived in Egypt between 1640 and 1532 B.C., which was a time of upheaval. It was introduced by people called the "Hyksos" ("rulers of foreign lands") who overran much of Egypt. The introduction of this speedy and maneuverable vehicle was a revolutionary breakthrough in the way that battles were fought. Pulled by two horses, the chariot was manned by one driver and one warrior. The warrior was armed with a spear, a shield and a bow. He was able to rain arrows on the enemy while his comrade urged the horses on. They *"speed forth and accomplish glorious deeds,"* one contemporary declared enthusiastically.

A *charioteer in action. Chariots were the most up-to-date battle technology of the time. They were also used for hunting.*

Chariot heroes

War chariots were crucial in battle. The soldiers who manned them were nicknamed "young heroes" and they quickly became the most important people in the army. Even pharaohs were proud to be thought of as charioteers. Many, such as young Pharaoh Tutankhamen (1333–1323 B.C.), were eager to have themselves pictured driving a war chariot, or to have boasts of their skill cut on the walls of their tombs. *"I commanded as chief of the chariots,"* declared Ramses II on a temple wall at Abydos.

Boomerangs and battering rams

Until the chariot revolution, Egyptian soldiers had to rely on fairly simple weapons. In the time before the pharaohs, the main weapons were bows and arrows, spears, axes, and maces. The mace was a crude but fearsome weapon – a stone club with a wooden handle. It was with weapons such as these that the soldiers of southern Egypt conquered the north and united the land in about 3000 B.C.. As a result, the first pharaohs liked to use the mace as a sign of their power, and it continued to be used in symbolic scenes right up until Roman times, 2,500 years later. Another weapon in use

at this time was a throw-stick (like a boomerang), a curved wooden blade that was thrown at the enemy. For attacking enemy towns or fortresses, battering rams and mobile towers were used.

A soldier wore no armor, but carried a large shield made of leather stretched over a wooden frame. Apart from this, his safety lay entirely in his skill with his weapons. At about the time of the chariot revolution, protection was increased with the introduction of tunics made of leather or linen and plated with strips of metal.

From about 1550 B.C. to 1070 B.C. the Egyptians tried to conquer people in Syria and Palestine. Sometimes as many as 20,000 Egyptian soldiers went into battle together. These model soldiers give us some idea of what they looked like.

Magic and mayhem

Pharaoh, his charioteers and other soldiers did not put all their hope in their weapons. They also turned to magic, believing that this would help bring victory. *"My enemy is under the soles of my feet,"* declared one magic spell to crush pharaoh's enemies. To give a magic boost to the process, pharaoh's enemies were shown on his footstool, on the flooring of his palace and on the soles of his sandals, so that they would be, quite literally, under his feet. Saying the right words, or miming what you wanted to happen, was thought to have the magic power to make it happen. For example, the names of enemy countries were written on pieces of pottery and, since pharaoh wanted to smash his enemies, that was what happened to the pottery: it was smashed. Archaeologists have found many pieces of broken pots, with enemy names written on them, at the sites of Egyptian forts.

This scene of African enemies being overcome by Egypt's army is from a chest made for Tutankhamen (1333–1323 B.C.).

Life in the army

According to one Egyptian writer, the soldier's life was all "blows," "beatings" and exhausting marches. Training was certainly tough, and commanders would order beatings for disobedient soldiers. The army was very well organized. Pharaoh was at its head. Below him, officers commanded smaller groups of soldiers. But fighting was not the soldier's only job. Pharaoh used the army to maintain his power at home, to guard trading missions and sometimes even to quarry stone and build the royal tomb.

THE DOCTOR

Thoth

Doctors in Egypt advised on all sorts of body care – even the making of deodorants. One prescription says:

To stop a man or woman's body stinking. Roast ostrich egg, tortoise shell, and gallnut from the tamarisk plant and rub the body with this mixture.

First-class doctors

Ancient Egypt was famed for the knowledge of its doctors. They were the most sophisticated doctors of their time. Some of the treatments they suggested have stood the test of time so well that they been used ever since – such as giving castor oil to help digestion. Egyptians were also very advanced in anatomy (understanding how the human body is made up). It was a long time before anyone bettered their knowledge.

There were many doctors in Egypt. Most were men, though a few women doctors do appear in the records. Some doctors were more important than others, and some specialized in treating certain types of illnesses. Pharaoh could call on "the king's eye doctor," "the doctor to the king's belly" and other specialists, for example. Sometimes all these titles were given to the same doctor, to show how skilled he was. One specialty area was gynecology (the study of women's bodies and the way babies are born). Here, a doctor's help could range from giving advice on how to have babies, to how to avoid having babies, to offering the world's first – almost reliable – pregnancy tests.

Egyptian thinking about illness was influenced by magic. The Egyptian bracelet pictured here takes us into this world of superstition. The eye on it was known as a "wadjet eye," which was supposed to represent the eye of the god Horus. It was thought to bring protection and stop the evil powers that brought illness.

31

Broken bones and crocodile dung

People who went to the doctor suffered from all sorts of illnesses, from diseases of the lungs, intestines, eyes and bones, to cancer. To help, the doctor might suggest an ointment or medicine. This might be made from rocks, animals, plants, herbs, or spices – for example, dates, garlic, or frankincense. There were more startling ingredients, too. *"Take crocodile dung and sour milk,"* advised one prescription. Doctors also treated wounds and broken bones. They examined wounds, made dressings for them, and set broken bones so they could mend.

Here, in a carving from a tomb, we can see one of the doctors of pharaoh Djoser (2630–2611 B.C.). His name was Hesire and he was known as "Chief of Dentists and Physicians." Hesire also had all sorts of other official titles.

But for all the good work of the doctors, most people had to accept a much lower standard of health and hygiene than we have today. Few people lived to be old, although we do know of some Egyptians who lived to be more than 90 years old. It was quite common to die at about the age of 36. Many babies died soon after they were born, or before their first birthday. Diseases were fairly common.

The wisdom of Thoth

Today we think of doctors as scientists: to the Egyptians, they were something far more powerful and important. They were experts with secret power to work magic and call on the gods. *"The doctor's guide is Thoth,"* explained an Egyptian book on medicine. Thoth was the scribes' god, the god of wisdom. Different gods and goddesses were thought to rule over each separate part of the doctor's work. The goddesses Hathor and Taweret governed childbirth. The goddess Isis protected the liver.

When you see how closely Egyptian medicine was connected to magic and religion, it will hardly surprise you to find out that doctors trained by studying at the most important temples in special centers called "Houses of Life." Here, they learned their job simply by reading what doctors before them had written.

Paintings and carvings from tombs can tell us about the sorts of illnesses that afflicted Egyptian people. Eye disease was a common problem, as this carving of a blind man playing a harp shows.

Papyrus, paintings and bones

There is evidence in all sorts of sources about the Egyptian doctors' work. Especially important are the writings left by the doctors themselves: problems and answers recorded on papyrus. Paintings from tombs show us doctors and patients. Also invaluable is the evidence on health and disease that scientists gain from looking at mummies, the bones of pharaoh and his people.

THE WOMAN

By reading the records of an Egyptian law court, we can eavesdrop on a well-born lady named Naunakhte as she looked back on her life:

I am a free woman of Egypt. I have raised eight children, and have given them everything suitable for their position in life. But now I have grown old, and see, my children don't look after me any more.

Portrait of a lady

A painting of a woman musician on a tomb wall. Most dancers, singers, and musicians in Egypt were women.

The picture Naunakhte painted of her life tells us a great deal about the way women were treated in ancient Egypt. They had a fair amount of freedom. They were not under the strict legal control of their husbands. The law allowed them to own property in their own right, and to make wills deciding who should have their belongings when they died. This was something Naunakhte certainly meant to take advantage of. *"I will give my goods to the children who* did *take care of me,"* she said in her will. But Naunakhte's story also tells us that there were important ways in which women were not free to do exactly as they wished. Most importantly, it was thought that the goal of every woman's life was to have a husband and children.

Given in marriage

Girls married at an early age. Brides were sometimes as young as eight or nine, though it was more usual to be married in the early teens. The husband was usually older than the bride, perhaps in his twenties.

Queen Nefertari making an offering to the gods. The Egyptians believed that ruling the country was man's work, and few women held power in their own right. Nefertari was a powerful woman. She was the favorite wife of Ramses II (1290–1224 B.C.) and had her own temple at Abu Simbel.

On one point most people agreed. It was much better for young people if their marriage partner was chosen by their parents and relatives. *"I have given to my slave the daughter of my sister as a wife,"* announced the head of one Egyptian family. It was obviously his job to do the matchmaking in his family. But it was usual for husband and wife to come from the same sort of background: noblemen married noblewomen, and peasants married peasants, for example. Matches between neighbors or even members of the same family were popular. Sometimes a pharaoh married his daughter or sister; for instance, Ramses II (1290–1224 B.C.) married his younger sister.

Sometimes a man had more than one wife – but that meant a good deal of expense. Pharaoh could afford many wives. But one wife was chosen as the most important from all the women in the royal harem (women's quarters). She was known as the

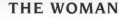
"Great Royal Consort" or "King's Great Wife." For example, Pharaoh Amenophis III (1391–1353 B.C.) chose Queen Tiy as his most important wife.

Married life

Once an Egyptian couple were married, the woman was expected to look after the house, and the man to provide for her. *"Start your household and love your wife. Fill her stomach with food and provide clothes for her back. Make her heart glad as long as you live,"* ran one piece of ancient wisdom. Wealthy women had servants for household tasks, from baking bread to cleaning and taking clothes to the river for washing. Other women had to do all this work in addition to helping their husbands. Peasant women helped their menfolk with the harvest, for example.

But the most important thing for any married woman was to have children. The advice many men were given was: *"Get a wife while you are young so she will give you a son."* Sons were more important than daughters, partly because they had a crucial role to play in the funeral ceremonies when their parents died. Children were useful in other ways, too: when they grew up they were expected to look after their parents, as we saw in Naunakhte's story at the start of this chapter.

This woman was a priestess who served the goddess Hathor. Hathor was especially associated with women.

Working women

Some women worked outside the home. Some worked as servants; some as weavers and spinners, making cloth; some in temples as musicians or priestesses; others as mourners who were hired to lament at funerals.

THE ARCHITECT

When Pharaoh Senwosret I (1971–1926 B.C.) decided it was time to build a new temple, the first person he had to choose was an architect. Scribes wrote down pharaoh's orders to his architect as follows:

Your advice will carry out everything my majesty wants to do. You are the one in charge. Order the workmen to act according to your plans.

Plans and calculations

Architects were the men in charge of pharaoh's great building works. Temples, tombs, pyramids, palaces, even new towns: these were the kinds of projects that called for an architect. His job started before any building work began. First of all, there were all sorts of plans and calculations to make.

To begin with, the architect had to plan the design of the building. Then there were practicalities to see to. From about 2630 B.C. onward, important buildings were built in stone. So the big question was: how much stone did the architect need? Then he had to decide where it was to come from, and how it was to be brought from the quarry to the building site. The answers to these questions meant working out another important piece of information: the number of workers needed. To obtain stone for one of Senwosret I's buildings, for example, more than 18,500 men were sent off to the quarries.

Pharaoh's scribes and other officials were on hand to help with the calculations. Sometimes these seemed to be endless, and to become

Egyptian statues were built to last forever. This statue of Pharaoh Djoser is about 4,700 years old. Djoser was buried beneath the first step pyramid (a pyramid shaped like a flight of steps).

increasingly sophisticated. The scribes had to work out how much food they would need for the workers, who were paid in rations rather than money. Once they had worked that out, another problem arose. The more important workers received more food. So how were the scribes to divide the food up into fractions of loaves and jugs of beer? The answer was to look up special sets of calculations. One of these helpfully explained the way *"to distribute 100 loaves among ten men when three men get double."*

Time to build

At last it was time to build. The architect was in charge of the hundreds of workers on site. There were unskilled workers to haul stone on rollers and sledges from the quarries to boats on the Nile, and from the boats to the building site. There were specialist workers: artists to paint scenes of the gods and the afterlife on tomb walls; sculptors to make statues for pyramids, tombs, and temples; goldsmiths and jewelers to decorate the statues. All these came under the architect's watchful eye.

Revolutions in stone

Using the skills of their architects, scribes and craftsmen, the Egyptians were some of the first people in the world ever to undertake massive building work in stone. Many of their creations have stood the test of time so well that they still exist today.

The tomb built for Pharaoh Djoser (2630–2611 B.C.) is a good example. The architect who designed the tomb created a completely new fashion for royal burials, which became popular for more than 1,000 years. His name was Imhotep, and his new design was the pyramid-shaped tomb. Djoser's tomb was

This statue shows Imhotep, the architect who designed the first step pyramid. People were so impressed by the pyramid, and by Imhotep's wisdom, that many years after his death he was honored as a god.

the first pyramid ever built. It was a "step pyramid," designed in the shape of a flight of steps.

Building on a grand scale

Finding out about the architect's job shows us the enormous scale of Egyptian building projects. And the projects themselves tell us about the power and wealth of the pharaohs. Anyone who lived in Egypt had to come and work for the king if they were summoned. Building work was often demanded from the ordinary people, especially when the Nile was flooding and farming had to stop.

Remembering the architects

Yet for all the amazing and record-breaking building work that pharaoh's architects planned, it was simply for their wisdom that the Egyptians liked to remember them. Imhotep went down in Egyptian history for his skill at medicine, rather than as an architect. But as far as any pharaoh was concerned, the best thing that could be said of an architect was that he was a good planner and organizer – a "royal master scribe."

Most pharaohs commissioned workers to start building their tombs as soon as they came to the throne. But who knew how long they had to do the work? Sometimes the pharaoh died before the tomb was finished and builders had to put down their tools so that pharaoh could be buried. Look at this picture. Do you think that the artist really meant to leave most of this wall unpainted?

THE TOMB-BUILDER

T he men who built tombs worked hard. And sometimes the day's work seemed too much. One complained to his supervisor:

I am just like a donkey to you ... If there is work to do, it's "find the donkey." It's a different story if there are extra rations.

Work, work, work

Over the centuries, builders worked on many different sizes and types of tombs. The most basic ones were burial places cut into cliffs or dug underground. But few people wanted a basic tomb. Pharaoh was the best example. He was the tomb-builders' main employer. To work for him on a tomb for the royal family was to be involved in the biggest and most spectacular project of all. Between about 2630 and 2134 B.C., tomb-builders worked on royal tombs in pyramid form. From around 1504 B.C. to 1070 B.C., they worked on royal burial sites in the Valley of the Kings, cutting deep into the cliffs to make tombs for pharaohs such as Tuthmosis I (1504–1492 B.C.).

But pharaoh was not the only one who called on the tomb-builders' skills. Craftsmen, such as the tomb-builders themselves, also wanted tombs. Priests, priestesses, well-born courtiers,

Tombs were scenes of great activity. While they were being built, they had all the hustle and bustle of a building site. This picture shows workers making mud bricks and smelting ore. When it was time to bury the tomb owner, a great procession of mourners arrived, wailing loudly. Later, family members or priests came regularly to the tomb to bring offerings to the deceased.

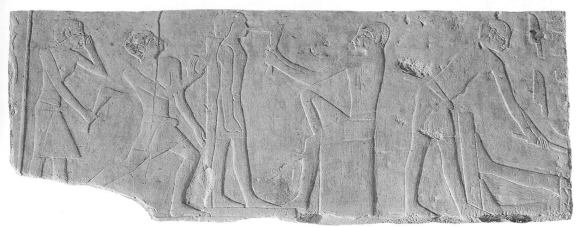

This busy scene shows sculptors at work making statues.

viziers, mayors, and other officials, important soldiers – all of them wanted tombs, and the best they could possibly afford. The best type of tomb had burial chambers below ground, with room for the mummies of a man, his wife, and their children, and all the goods that the dead were thought to need in the afterlife. The tomb of Pharaoh Tutankhamen (1333–1323 B.C.), for example, was packed with possessions, from gaming boards to war chariots, and from sandals and underclothing to jars of wine and flower garlands. Above ground level, the tomb-builders put up a small chapel called the mortuary chapel, where special religious ceremonies for the dead took place.

Building for another world

Many different types of craftsmen worked on the tombs. First of all, laborers and stone masons did the actual construction work – quarrying, shaping stone, building, digging and tunneling into the rock. Then plasterers came along to smooth the tomb walls with a coating of plaster. Next, draftsmen marked out the pictures that were to be painted on the walls, carefully dividing the surface into squares so that their figures would be the right size. Artists came to paint them. Sculptors arrived to make statues of the tomb-owners.

Building tombs called for all sorts of skills – from plastering to make the walls smooth to painting. Tombs were decorated with religious scenes and pictures of everyday life. This tomb painting shows a foreman of the tomb-builders worshiping a phoenix (a sacred bird).

At last the builders could stand back and admire the finished tomb, glowing with painted walls and inhabited with life-size statues. Like all Egyptians, they believed that the paintings and statues were not simply decoration – they had magic power. Paintings in the tomb of a craftsman called Sennedjem, for instance, showed goddesses protecting Sennedjem's mummy. Painting the scene was expected to make it come true, so that goddesses would look after Sennedjem.

Time on ... time off

Many clues about the builders' life and work come from a village called Deir el-Medina built especially for Pharaoh Tuthmosis I's tomb-builders. Records from the village show us that the men were very closely supervised. Scribes checked that they turned up to work and noted down absentees. "Eye trouble," "embalming mother," "taking donkey to vet" and "brewing beer" were just some of the excuses for a day off. Foremen inspected the quality of work. Other officials handed out tools and equipment and later checked them back in.

The last day of the month was pay day. The Egyptians did not use coins, so wages were in goods – grain, beer, fish, and other items. The villagers of Deir el-Medina received a good wage by Egyptian standards.

THE SERVANT

Servants were a vital part of the Egyptian work-force. They were treated strictly. One popular saying was:

A servant who does not get beaten will have angry thoughts in his heart.

Dust, mice, and fleas

Many people in ancient Egypt worked as servants, men and women alike. There was plenty of work for them, for no well-to-do household was without its staff of servants.

Domestic tasks were high on the list of jobs that servants had to do. Cleaning was a daily job, and it all had to be done by hand, such as sweeping out the rooms with a brush. It wasn't just a question of tackling dust – there was a whole horde of un-wanted intruders to keep out, even in the best-kept homes: flies, mosquitoes, bedbugs, fleas, lizards, snakes, rats, and mice. It was the servants' job to deal with all these. Any help they wanted had to be made at home. For example, they would make a

Servants hard at work indoors, making beds. This picture was carved in about 2400 B.C. It tells us that some daily chores have been the same for thousands of years.

A tomb painting showing servants picking grapes from a vine. Grapes were used for making wine.

spray out of the chemical natron, to kill fleas. All sorts of handy household hints were passed on between the servants. *"Stop mice coming in. Smear everything with cat grease,"* was one. *"Stop a snake coming out of its hole – plug an onion in it,"* was another.

When this work was done, there were heavier cleaning jobs, too. One was getting rid of household waste, for there was no sewage system and no refuse collection. Most waste was dumped in a nearby canal, or simply in the street. This attracted mice and rats, and so made more work for the servants the next day. Another task was fetching water. There was no running water, and few houses had wells for water. All the water needed for cooking, washing, and cleaning had to be brought each day from the nearest canal or from the Nile River.

Women's work

Some servants, especially women, were given work looking after the master or mistress of the house. The women were expected to have many skills – as beauticians, hairdressers, and masseuses. After a session with her personal servants, one mistress remembered, *"My hair was combed. I was dressed in the finest linen. I was anointed with perfumed oil."* Servants even provided showers for their employers, pouring water over the bather's head, while standing behind a screen to give the bather privacy.

Everyone works for pharaoh

Being a servant meant hard work. But servants were free people. They were paid for their work, and were by no means the least important people in the land. Egyptians did not think that working as a servant was something to be ashamed of. After all, everyone had to work for pharaoh.

Slaves

The work of Egyptian slaves was very like that of the servants. Women cooked, cleaned, and shopped; the men worked in the gardens and fields. But there was one very big difference between servants and slaves. Slaves were not free. They belonged to their **master** or mistress and could be sold like any other piece of property.

There were never very many slaves in Egypt, partly because pharaoh could demand work from his own people whenever he wanted. But numbers began to rise from about 1550 B.C. onward, when Egypt began to launch a series of successful foreign wars, and prisoners were brought home to work as slaves.

This servant is making beer – a daily job that took a great deal of time. Models of servants and other workers were often put in tombs. They were expected to come to life and work for the tomb owner in the next life.

Serving forever

The work of servants and slaves was such a part of everyday life that the Egyptians couldn't imagine ever doing without them. When they thought about life after death, they were sure they would need servants then, too. Many tombs contained models of servants at work. With the help of a little magic, these figures were expected to come to life and do their masters' and mistresses' heavy work for all eternity.

GLOSSARY

Amun The chief state-god of Egypt. Usually associated with Re, the sun god, and also called Amun-Re.

Anubis A god with the head of a jackal, thought to be in charge of embalming and watching over burial grounds.

Architect An important royal official in charge of a building project.

Demotic The everyday writing of Egypt used from about 700 B.C. to 400 A.D.

Embalmer Someone who preserves dead bodies. The Egyptians did this by making mummies.

Hieratic Type of "joined-up" Egyptian writing, used mainly for religious texts.

Hieroglyphics Egyptian system of writing using picture signs. It was very elaborate and required much careful practice.

Horus A god with a human body and the head of a hawk. He was the son of Osiris and identified with the living pharaoh.

House of Life Place of learning attached to an important temple.

Inscription Words cut in stone, often recording important events.

Isis A goddess; the wife and sister of the god Osiris.

Ka One of the spirit parts of a person, like a "double," thought to live on after death.

Lower Egypt The north of Egypt, joined to the south in about 3000 B.C..

Mortuary chapel A chapel built at a tomb. Offerings of food and drink were made to the spirit of the dead person here.

Mummy A dead body that had been dried out, treated with preservatives, and wrapped in linen bandages.

Natron A chemical with many uses; for example, preserving dead bodies.

Nomarch The governor of a nome.

Nome One of the administrative areas into which Egypt was divided.

Osiris An important Egyptian god, thought to rule the land of the dead.

Papyrus (plural, **papyri**) A reed, or a sheet of writing material made from the reed.

Pharaoh King of the Egyptians.

Pyramid A style of tomb built for a member of the royal family.

Re One of the names of the sun god.

Scribe A man who could write, who worked keeping records and accounts.

Step pyramid A pyramid shaped like a flight of steps.

Thoth A god with a human body and the head of an ibis (a bird with a long beak). Thoth was the god of wisdom and writing.

Upper Egypt The south of Egypt, joined to the north in about 3000 B.C.

Vizier Pharaoh's chief official.

FURTHER READING

Corbishley, Mike, *Pathways: Timelines of the Ancient World*, Macdonald Young Books, 1995.

Defrates, Joanna, *What Do We Know About Egyptians?*, Macdonald Young Books, 1994.

Hart, George, *Eyewitness Ancient Egypt*, Dorling Kindersley, 1990.

Howarth, Sarah, *The Unfolding World – The Pyramid Builders*, Quarto/Running Press 1993.

The Visual Dictionary of Ancient Civilizations, Dorling Kindersley, 1994.

INDEX